Includes Five
SAT
Words to Know
MEETS STATE AND NATIONAL STANDARDS
India
Land of Six Senses and Intriguing Mystery!
IT'S YOUR WORLD
LIVE
WORK
PLAY
LEARN
Where Do You Want to Go?
TIME ZONE • CULTURE • CUSTOMS • CLOTHING • HISTORY
CLOTHING • HISTORY
Hey! It's the
Taj Mahal!
Do you want to go?
FOOD • CULTURE • CUSTOMS • CLOTHING • HISTORY • LANDMARKS
By Carole Marsh

Live • Work • Play • Learn

GALLOPADE INTERNATIONAL

Gallopade International is introducing SAT words that kids need to know in our books. The SAT words in this book have a gray box around them. Students can look up the definitions and increase their vocabulary. Happy Learning!

Gallopade is proud to be a member and supporter of these educational organizations and associations:

Association for the Study of African American Life and History
National Alliance of Black School Educators
American Booksellers Association
American Library Association
International Reading Association
National Association for Gifted Children
The National School Supply and Equipment Association
The National Council for the Social Studies
Museum Store Association
Association of Partners for Public Lands
Association of Booksellers for Children

At the time of publication, all websites referenced in this document were valid. However, due to the changing nature of the Internet, some addresses may change or the content become less relevant.

It's Your World Books

Africa: A Safari Through Its Amazing Nations!

Australia: The Land Down Under for Mates of All Ages!

Canada: The Maple Leaf Melting Pot Country!

China: A Great Wall Runs Thru It!

Egypt: An Ancient Land of Lore; a Modern Land of Oil and More!

France: The Ooh-La-La Country Everyone Loves!

Germany: The Country of Fairytale Castles and Cutting Edge Science!

Greece: A Volcanic Land of Ancient Olympic Origins!

India: Land of Six Senses and Intriguing Mystery!

Italy: The Country of Amazing Fountains and Awesome Arts!

Japan: An Island Country of Endless Intrigue!

Mexico: A Colorful Land of Exotic Culture!

Middle East: Ancient Countries of Current Events Headlines!

Russia: The Great Bear and Its Dramatic History!

South America: A Continent of Countries of Amazing Proportions!

United Kingdom: The Country of Ships, Sealing Wax, Cabbages, and Kings!

Other Carole Marsh Related Titles:

Fantasy Field Trips: Adventure to the Eight Wonders of the World!

Table of Contents

A Letter from the Author

From the desk of
CAROLE MARSH

Hey kids,

It's your world! It really, really is!
Of course, you already know that, don't you?
You surf the 'net, listen to satellite radio, watch television shows and movies set all around the globe–kids today are much more "worldly" than in the past, and that's a good thing!

Now's a great time to learn something about another country–such as India. Why? Because one day, you might actually visit there (if you have not already!). You might go to school there–many colleges have ties with international schools around the globe. You might even go on to work in a foreign country!

Many companies have positions in other countries. Companies are "going global" as fast as they can. They have branch offices, manufacturing plants, and customer service centers scattered around the globe!

So, ready or not: YOU are a Citizen of the World! And you'll want to be a good one. How do you do that? You'll find out everything you can about that country, how it's the same, and how it's different from your own country. What language is spoken there? What customs do the people observe? What foods do they enjoy? What do they do for fun? What has happened in this part of the world, and what is happening there now? It's fun ... and the more you learn, the more you will enjoy whatever global opportunity comes your way!

This book is a good place to start your learning journey–so take advantage of the world– IT'S YOUR WORLD, after all ... and guess what? It's a BIG world, after all!

Happy traveling and learning,

Carole Marsh
Always with passport in hand!

Why Should We Care About India?

India is located in the southern part of the Asian continent and is Asia's second largest country, after China. India is just over one-third the size of the United States, but it has more than three times the number of people! India is set apart from the rest of Asia by the Himalayas. Reaching more than 8,000 meters (26,000 feet) above sea level, the Himalayan Mountains contain the highest mountain ranges in the world.

For the traveler, India offers a great variety of landscapes, from mountains, lake regions, and forests in the north, to the beautiful beaches and rain forests of western India. The Taj Mahal, located in Uttar Pradesh, is considered one of the Seven Wonders of the World and is visited by millions of people every year.

One day, you might visit India and take a boat ride on the Ganges River, attend a Hindu wedding in Mumbai, study at the Indian Institute of Technology in Delhi, or work for a company in Bangalore. It could happen!

Write home about it!
What will your postcard from India say?

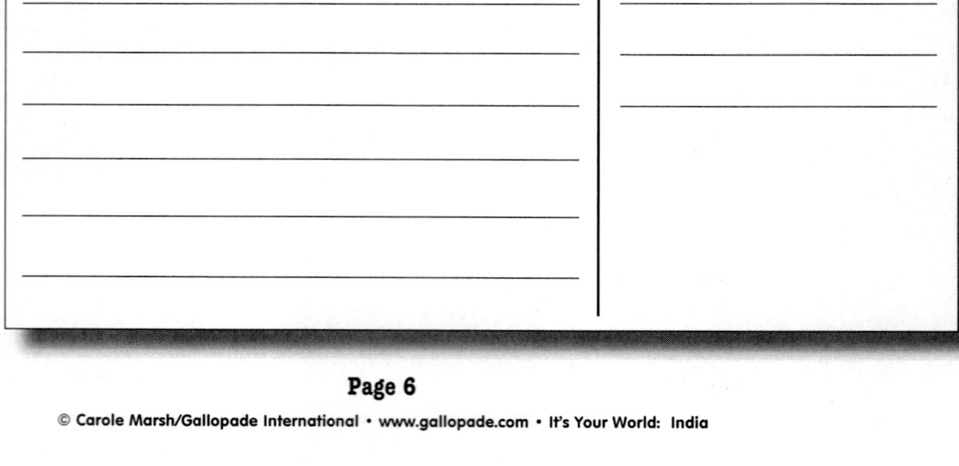

Top Fast India Facts

Important facts to remember about the country of India:

- India's national emblem is the *Sarnath Lion Capital of Ashoka.*
- The currency used in India is called the *rupee.*
- India's form of government is parliamentary and includes executive, legislative, and judiciary branches.
- Seventeen different major languages and 844 separate dialects are spoken in India.
- The country of India consists of 28 states and seven union territories.
- The national bird of India is the peacock.
- The president of India is Pratibha Devisingh Patil. She is the first woman to be elected to the office.
- India has the fourth largest economy in the world.
- On August 15, 1947, the country of India became independent from British rule.
- The national anthem of India is *Jana Gana Mana* (Thou Art the Ruler of All Minds).

Now, you figure out the rest!

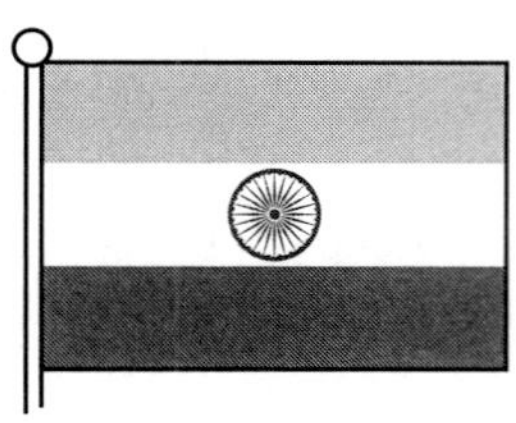

1. This is the Indian ___ ___ ___ ___ .

2. The ___ ___ ___ ___ ___ ___ ___ ___ ___ ___ of India is more than 1.1 billion people.

3. A large percentage of Indian people are ___ ___ ___ ___ ___ ___ ___ ___ ___ ___ and therefore don't eat meat.

4. The ___ ___ ___ ___ ___ religion is practiced by 80 percent of the people in India.

5. Like Hollywood, Bollywood in Mumbai is the ___ ___ ___ ___ ___ capital of India.

6. The *sari* is one of the most common ___ ___ ___ ___ ___ ___ ___ ___ worn by women in India.

Where in the World Is India?

- India is located in the southern part of Asia.
- India borders Bangladesh, Bhutan, Burma, China, Nepal, and Pakistan.
- The capital city of India is New Dehli.
- India's coastline borders the Arabian Sea and the Bay of Bengal, between Burma and Pakistan.
- Kanchenjunga, the third tallest mountain in the world, lies on the border with Nepal and is India's highest elevation.

- From its most northern point on the border of China, India extends approximately 2000 miles to its most southern point just above Sri Lanka.
- 17 percent of the world's population lives in India on just slightly more than 2.4 percent of the total world land mass.
- Until 1896, India was the only known source of diamonds in the world.
- The Baily Bridge is the highest bridge in the world. It is located in the Ladakh Valley between the Dras and Suru Rivers in the Himalayan Mountains.

Do You Know?

1. India exports computer software to:
a. 30 countries b. 63 countries c. 27 countries d. 90 countries

2. The largest employer in the world is Indian Railways. They have:
a. 100 employees b. 2,000 employees c. 1 million employees d. 68,000 employees

Ancient History

Civilization has existed in India since approximately 2600 B.C.E. One of the earliest known Indian civilizations inhabited the Indus River Valley. Cities of the Indus River Valley were made of brick and stone. They also contained water wells and drainage systems which were some of the most sophisticated of the ancient world. This civilization eventually declined and ended by 1700 B.C.E., due to a lack of available water.

The Aryan civilization, which described itself as "the noble ones," controlled India from about 1700 to 1000 B.C.E. The Aryans were a tribal people who were ruled by a war-chief, or *raja* (king). Invading from northern lands, they controlled India after successfully conquering all of the Persian territories.

From the 17th century to the middle of the 20th century, India was ruled by the British Empire. Led by Mahatma Gandhi, India finally gained independence from Britain in 1947.

Crosswords!

Use your new knowledge to fill in the crossword puzzle.

Across

3. The word *raja* means _____.
4. One of the earliest civilizations was found in the _________ River Valley.
5. India was led by Mahatma _________ and gained independence from Britain in 1947.

Down

1. From the 17th century to the middle of the 20th century, India was ruled by the ______ Empire.
2. The Aryans conquered the _______ territories.
6. The ______ civilization ruled India from 1700 to 1000 B.C.E.

Peaceful Independence!

Gandhi

The British presence in India dates back to the early part of the 17th century! In 1757, a British company called the East India Trading Company transformed itself from an association of traders to rulers of India. The Indian people were frustrated under British rule and in 1857 the Indian Rebellion broke out. The rebellion was crushed by Britain, but it led to the formation of an Indian National Congress. The Congress worked to give the people of India more power.

In 1919, 400 unarmed Indian people were killed by British soldiers. A man named Mahatma Gandhi became the leader of India's struggle for freedom. Gandhi believed in peaceful, nonviolent protest instead of war, using hunger strikes and prayer to make his point. Under his unofficial leadership, Great Britain finally granted India independence in 1947.

Timeline!
Number these events in the order that they took place, first to last.

___ British East India Trading Company transforms into rulers of India.

___ The Indian National Congress forms.

___ The Indian Rebellion breaks out.

___ Mahatma Gandhi becomes leader of India's struggle for freedom.

___ India is granted independence.

___ The Indian Rebellion ends.

___ Famous massacre of 400 unarmed Indian people occurs.

Interesting Indians!

Matching!

Match these famous Indian people with their accomplishments:

______1. I was born in Porbander in western India in 1869. Through nonviolence and peaceful resistance, I led India to independence from Great Britain. I am known as the Father of the Indian Nation.

______2. Of Albanian descent and born in 1910, I became a Roman Catholic nun and devoted myself to working with the poor in the slums of Calcutta, India. I became famous throughout the world as an advocate for the poor. I was awarded the Nobel Peace Prize in 1979.

______3. Although I am known by a different name, my birth name was Siddhartha Gautama. I was born into royalty around 563 B.C.E. in Nepal. My teachings are the basis of one of the major world religions.

______4. I became the president of the Indian National Congress in 1959 and India's prime minister in 1966 and again in 1980. Under my leadership, India became victorious in the India-Pakistan War in 1971. After I was assassinated by my own bodyguard in 1984, my son Rajiv became prime minister.

______5. I was born in Bengal in 1887 and became one of the most influential painters of the 20th century. My paintings were inspired by the everyday life of the people of Bengal.

______6. I play the *sitar*, which is a traditional Indian string instrument that has been used for hundreds of years. I made many significant contributions in popularizing classical Indian music, especially through my recordings with George Harrison of the Beatles. I have won two Grammy Awards.

A. Ravi Shankar

B. Indira Gandhi

C. Mother Teresa

D. Jamini Roy

E. Gandhi

F. Buddha

Guts and Glory Indian Style!

A. Between 1896 and 1921, it killed over 10 million people in India. It is usually contracted through the bite of infected insects or animals, such as fleas or rats, which spread its bacteria. It gets its name from the black lumps and spots that appear on the neck, chest, arms, and legs of the human body.

____

B. These events, which are caused by a lack of rainfall, have resulted in extreme famine and the death of millions of Indian people over time. This one lasted from 1876 to 1878 and resulted in the death of more than five million people from starvation and disease.

____

C. These animals are worshiped and have been considered sacred by the Hindus in India for over 5,000 years! They are allowed to roam free on city streets and are considered to be part of the family in many cases. It is against Indian law to hurt or kill this animal.

____

D. This places a huge strain on available water, food, and resources in many of India's largest cities.

____

E. He was known as Netaji by the people of India and was one of the most influential politicians in modern Indian history. He opposed Mahatma Gandhi's nonviolent approach to gaining freedom from Britain.

____

Mixed Up!
Match the paragraph to the word or phrase that the paragraph describes.

DROUGHT _____

_____ **CITY OVERCROWDING**

BLACK PLAGUE _____

UBHAS CHANDRA BOSE _____

COWS THOUGHT TO BE RELATIVES _____

A Leathery Performance!

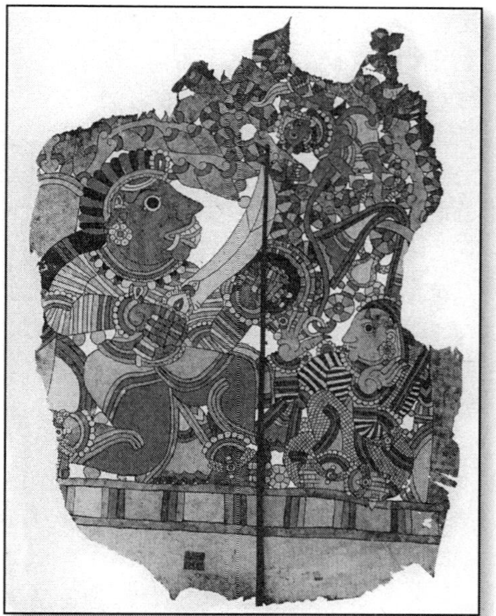
Indian Leather Puppet

Do you like to play with puppets? Indians have loved puppetry for many years. In the early days, puppets in India were based on characters in Hindu mythology and used to tell their stories. Flat and usually made of leather, they were carved with a lot of detail. After they were finished, they were hung on a rope behind a see-through screen made of cloth. The bright light from an oil lamp was used to project them onto the screen and a puppet show was created!

Before the start of television or movies, shadow puppetry was a popular form of entertainment in India. Puppeteers and their families traveled from village to village to perform their shows. All family members would participate in the performance of the puppet show, providing voices for each male, female, and child character. Music was also an important part of the performance.

While movies and television have replaced shadow puppetry in most parts of India, there are still festivals that use the art form today!

Write your own puppet show!
Get out your pencil or pen. Write a brief fictional story that could be performed using puppets!

Talk to the Animals!

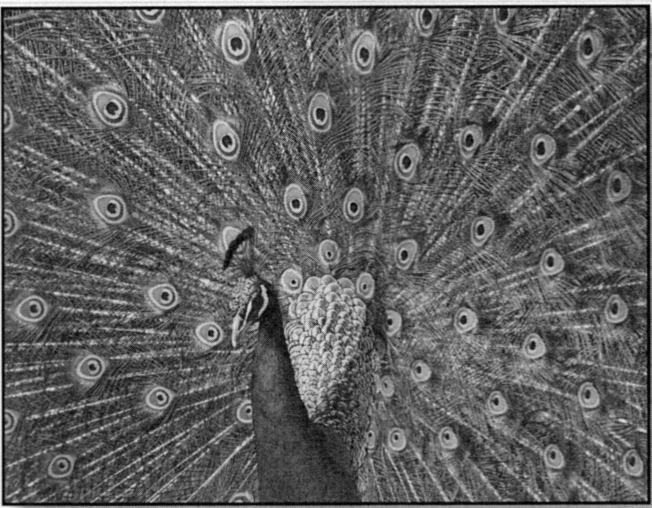

Peacock

Animals are very important in Indian religion and culture! The peacock and elephant are two examples. The peacock, a symbol of love, grace, beauty, and joy, is the national bird of India. It appears in many forms of Indian art and literature. In the Hindu religion, Lord Krishna is commonly depicted with the peacock or wearing a headdress of peacock feathers. It is believed that when the peacock fans its beautiful feathers, the rains will follow.

The elephant, a symbol of power and wisdom, is also an important part of Indian religion. The Hindu god Ganesha is traditionally shown as having an elephant's head, and a pot-bellied human body.

Animals are an important part of the culture of India. Its people believe that every form of life, including wildlife, should be treated with great respect.

Word Play!
Use the letters from the words elephant and peacock to make as many words with three letters or more as you can.

ELEPHANT PEACOCK

Ganesha

The Taj Mahal, A Site to See!

The Taj Mahal is one of the most beautiful buildings in the world! It is a mausoleum, or a large tomb. It was commissioned by Emperor Shah Jahan for his favorite wife, Empress Mumtaz Mahal, who died in 1631. Shah Jahan loved his wife Mumtaz so much that he ordered the building of the most beautiful mausoleum on Earth. It took 22 years to build! It was built by a workforce of 22,000 that included laborers, painters, stonecutters, gardeners, embroidery artists, and masons.

The construction of the Taj Mahal took 22 years.

The name Taj Mahal means “Crown Palace” or “Crown of the Palace.”

Some say that Shah Jahan ordered that the hands of the craftsmen and architect be chopped off after building the Taj Mahal, because he did not want them to build another monument as grand as this one.

The Taj Mahal is considered to be the seventh wonder of the world. Do you know the other six?

For the transportation of the construction materials, more than 1,000 elephants were used.

Create your very own travel pamphlet. Concentrate on an area that interests you. Perhaps you enjoyed learning about the people. Or maybe it was the monuments that interested you. Fold a piece of paper into three sections. This will give you six areas on which to put information.

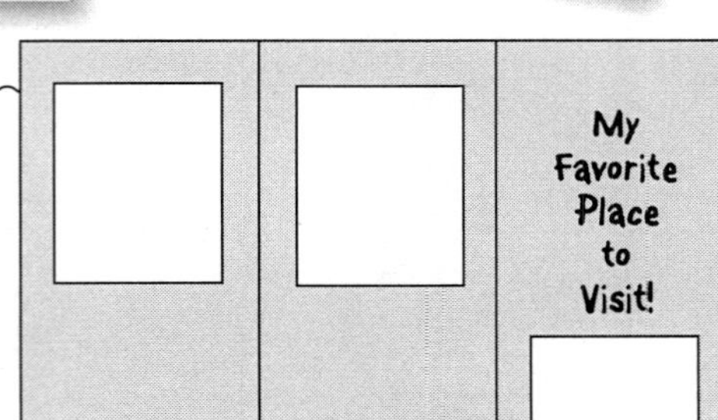

It's Customary

Customs and culture vary widely from country to country. Sometimes they vary in different regions of the same country. Here are customs and cultural differences observed by the people of India!

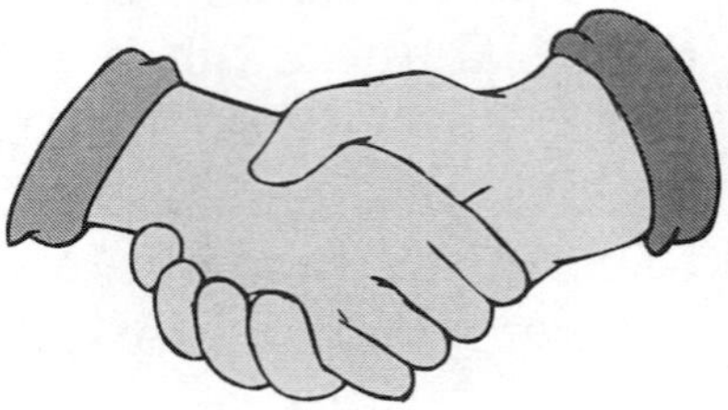

- The handshake is a common greeting in India, but men and women seldom shake hands with each other.
- It is considered very rude to tell someone "no" or to even express "no."
- The different groups of people in India use names differently. A Hindu's formal name would be their name, then "son of" or "daughter of," followed by their father's name. Your formal name might be Joe, son of Joseph!
- Never give someone white flowers as a gift, since they are associated with funerals.
- If you are offered a drink or snack at someone's house, you should say "no" the first time. When your host offers a second time, you can accept!
- It's often OK to eat with your hands, but you should only use your right hand!
- Indian women wear colorful garments called *saris*. A *sari* is a long, wide scarf that is wrapped around the body and shoulder.
- Indian food is very spicy. Potatoes or rice are part of almost every meal.

Create your own!

Customs and cultural activities can help define who we are. Think about your family and friends and come up with some new customs for everyone to try.

Hindi? Where's That From?

The official language in India is Hindi. They use a different alphabet. Their alphabet is the Devanagari.

Match it up!
Below are some common Hindi phrases or words. See if you can match them to the English word.

badan	sun
munh	big
naam	above
haath	mouth
tamatar	day
lamba	name
upar	hand
din	rice
bara	long
suraj	tomato

Happy Holidays!

A festival is celebrated almost every day somewhere in India! Each small village has its own special celebrations. There are also big festivals celebrated throughout the country. Many of these festivals are part of the Hindu religion.

Holi is a Hindu festival that celebrates the arrival of spring. People throw colored water or powder on each other. They believe that the bright colors will scare away evil spirits. Another festival is **Diwali**, or the Hindu New Year. For five days, people will dress up and exchange presents.

India also has several national holidays. **Republic Day**—January 26th—celebrates the day India became a republic. **Independence Day** is celebrated on August 15th. This is the day that India became independent from Great Britain.

Write it down!
Pretend that you are visiting India and have just seen a great festival. Write a letter to your best friend. Write about what you have seen. Describe what people were wearing and what they were doing.

India on the Stage and in the Museums!

The exotic art and music of India is deeply rooted in tradition and religion. Indian culture is made up of various forms of rhythmic music, dance, tribal art, and body art.

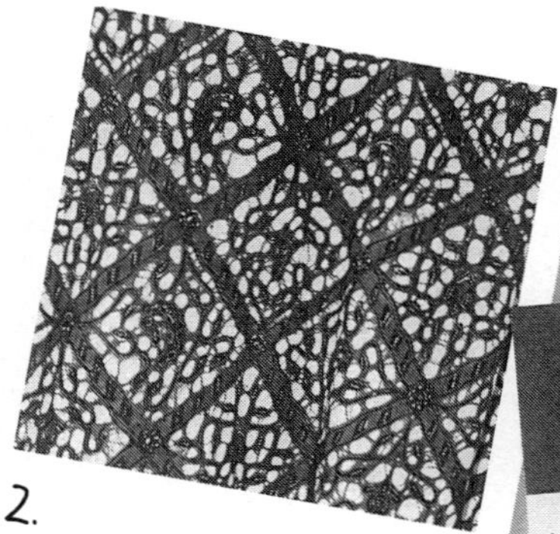

2.

3.

Notes

1. The *bindi* has become an artistic symbol of beauty and culture for the women of India.

2. *Batik* is a craft technique achieved by using cracked wax and dye on cloth.

3. *Bharatanatyam* dancers reflect varying moods through their eyes, hands, and feet.

4. *Tanjore* folk art is decorated with semi-precious stones, pearls, glass, and gold.

5. The 80-foot Great Buddha Statue in India was created to spread the message of Buddhism and world peace.

1.

5.

4.

What's for Dinner?

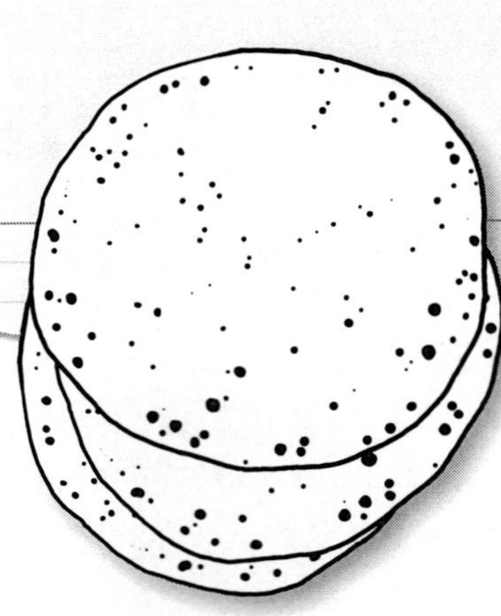

Indians cook with a lot of different spices, such as saffron, cinnamon, and cumin. Some of these spices make the food hot, while others are mild. Curry powder is a combination of several different spices. Take a look below at some common Indian dishes.

Chapati is a round, flat wheat bread. It is quite common and looks like a tortilla.

Basmati rice is nutty-smelling and is served with many different kinds of dishes.

Dal is a stew made of lentils.

Curry can be a spicy sauce served with meats and vegetables. *Curry* is also a spicy stew!

RECIPE

Always ask an adult for help when cooking!

MMMMMMM...this was good!

Raita

INGREDIENTS

1 large cucumber
2 1/2 cups yogurt
1/2 teaspoon salt
8 to 10 slices flat bread (pita bread)

DIRECTIONS

Grate the cucumber with a hand grater or in a food processor.
Place the grated cucumber in a strainer, drain, and squeeze out the excess moisture.
With a spoon, mix cucumber, yogurt, and salt in a medium bowl.
Tear flat bread into small pieces for dipping and serve.

Makes 15 to 20 servings

Run, Chase!

Field Hockey

India's national sport may be field hockey and its favorite sport cricket, but a uniquely Indian sport is something called Kho Kho! The sport was invented at the beginning of the 20th century and the first official rules were published in 1924. Each Kho Kho game consists of two teams with 12 players each. It lasts for two innings that are each seven minutes long. Only nine players from each team are allowed on the field at the same time. The object of the game is to tag all of your opponents in the shortest possible time by touching them with the palm of your hand. The quickest team wins!

Figure it out!

1. If a Kho Kho match has two innings that last seven minutes each, how much time does it take to play a whole game?

____

2. In Kho Kho there are 12 players on each team, but only nine from each side are allowed on the field at the same time. How many players in total are left over?

____

Kho Kho

Fast Fact:
The Kho Kho Federation of India (K.K.F.I.) is the primary governing body of the game in India.

Mumbai–Lights, Camera, Bollywood!

The people of India love movies! Mumbai is the movie capital of India, Bollywood. Does that sound like another place famous for making movies? Of course it does! It's called Hollywood! You might be surprised to know that Bollywood actually produces more movies every year than Hollywood does!

The name Bollywood was created using the "B" from Mumbai's original name, Bombay, and adding "ollywood", in tribute to the U.S. film capital. Very clever!

Mumbai (Bombay at that time) began as seven small islands inhabited by Koli fishermen. Townships and trade ports were soon built. In 1534, the Portuguese took control of the land. In 1661, the islands became a wedding gift from the Portuguese to King Charles II of England when he married Catherine of Braganza.

By the middle of the 19th century, industries including textile mills, docks, and railways began to attract immigrants looking for jobs. This began a wild growth in the population of India, which continues today!

In 1995, Bombay's name was changed to Mumbai. Today, it is one of the world's largest cities, with an estimated population of 14 million people!

Word Fun!

Match the name of the historical landmark with the type of attraction it is.

Hanging Gardens, Mahalaxmi Temple, Haji Ali Mausoleum, Sanjay Gandhi National Park, Nehru Planetarium, Prince of Wales Museum, Siddhivinayak Temple

Temple / Mosque	Historical / Nature	Museum

India Did It First!

Did I Miss Any?
Buttons, made from seashells, originated in India around 2000 B.C.E. They were mostly used as ornaments at that time.

Like My New Sweater?
The first written mention of using Cashmere wool for clothing occurred in the 3rd century. Shawls were made from it in the Kashmir region of India.

Water Your Plants!
The crescograph, a device used to measure growth in plants, was invented in the early 20th century by Jagdish Chandra Bose, a Bengali scientist.

Word Fun!
This is fun to do with someone else. Ask a friend for words to substitute for the blanks in the story. Their word substitutions will have a humorous effect when the resulting story is then read aloud.

I want to be the first person to ______________ (ACTION VERB)

across ______________ (COUNTRY)! I've been training for this

since ______________ (MONTH). I'm in ______________ (ADJECTIVE) shape.

My ______________ (ADJECTIVE) adventure will begin on

______________ (FAVORITE HOLIDAY). I won't be hard to miss;

I'll be the one wearing a ______________ (COLOR)

______________ (ARTICLE OF CLOTHING) and a pair of matching

______________ (FOOTWEAR). My faithful friends

______________ (FAMOUS ATHLETE) and

______________ (CARTOON CHARACTER) will be there to cheer for me.

I'm bringing my ______________ (NOUN) along for good luck.

I'm confident I'll be the first!

2, 4, 6, 8, Who Do We Appreciate?
The modern decimal number system originated in India in the 9th century.

Wear Your Carats!
Diamonds were first used as gemstones in central India. India was the only major source of diamonds in the world until they were discovered in Brazil.

It's Your Move!
One of the earliest board games known to man, Pachisi, originated in India in the 6th century. Pachisi was played by the Mughal emperors of India.

Time to Plant the Corn!
The earliest evidence of an animal-drawn plow, used to clear fields for planting, was found in India.

"Caste" in Stone!

Achuta

Life can be tough in India! If a child is born into the Hindu religion, he or she is automatically part of what is called a "caste system." The caste system embraces the belief that all men are *not* created equal.

A part of India's culture for centuries, the caste system places all people into a variety of specific classes.

Brahman

These four social classes include the *Brahmans* (priests and teachers); *Kshatriyas* (rulers and soldiers); *Vaisyas* (merchants and traders); and *Sudras* (laborers). A fifth group includes the people who are *achuta*, or outcasts. They are limited to doing unpleasant and menial jobs.

To this day, the quality of your education, the jobs that are made available to you, and who you will be allowed to marry still depends on your caste level. As India continues to grow and evolve, progress is being made toward stopping the discrimination that exists in the caste system!

Fast Fact:
The Hindu religion is observed by more than 80 percent of India's population.

Questions, Questions!

Write 5 questions about the types of jobs that are associated with each Indian social caste.

Example: What kind of jobs would a Sudra do?

1. ______________________________?

2. ______________________________?

3. ______________________________?

4. ______________________________?

5. ______________________________?

Tiger Terrain!

Bengal Tiger

Did you know that India has created a safe haven for tigers? The Sunderbans National Park is home to one of the most magnificent animals on the planet—the Bengal tiger! The Sunderbans, where the Ganges River meets the Indian Ocean, is made up of the largest river delta and mangrove forest in the world. It provides the perfect habitat for the Bengal tiger, which is also known as the Indian tiger.

During the 20th century, several species of tigers became extinct. As a result, the Bengal tiger was labeled an endangered species. In 1973, a tiger reserve was established in the Sunderbans to protect and provide a natural habitat for Bengal tigers.

Sunderbans National Park

An adult Bengal tiger can weigh up to 550 pounds and can measure nearly nine feet from its head to the tip of its tail. Now, that's a big cat! Today, over 250 of these beautiful creatures reside in the Sunderbans National Park and need to continue to be protected to ensure that the species survives.

Revealing Answer!

Follow the instructions to reveal the type of forest that exists in the Sunderbans.

1. Cross off the first two letters.
2. Cross off the letter "W."
3. Cross off the sixth and seventh letter.
4. Cross off the 11th letter.
5. Cross off the 14th letter.
6. Cross off the last three letters.

Z A M W A T Y N G R L O V K E B Z P

India's "Great" War!

Mounted Elephant

In the history of wars, nothing comes close to the surprise that the Indian army gave Alexander the Great. What was their secret weapon? Elephants!

India has fought many wars throughout the centuries. One of the most famous was King Porus' battle against Alexander the Great of Macedonia. In 327 B.C.E., Alexander, considered one of the most successful military commanders of all time, marched his army into Punjab, to conquer India. But King Porus was ready for war! He positioned his army on the east bank of the Hydapes River to prevent Alexander and his army from crossing into India.

The Macedonians knew they outmatched the smaller Indian army. But they had no plan to deal with King Porus' elephants! He had cleverly positioned the elephants between his troops and the Macedonians, knowing their horses would be afraid of the huge animals!

Alexander the Great

In the end, the Indian army was defeated and King Porus was captured. Alexander, as he had done with other rulers he defeated, allowed Porus to continue to govern his territory and later gave him another province as a gift. The elephants paid off after all!

Cross it off!

Starting with the first letter, cross off every other letter to reveal the river named in the story.

X H S Y Q D Z A L P L E I S

____

Bangalore, the Outsourcing Capital!

Infosys Headquarters, India

If you're having trouble with your computer and call the information line for help, don't be surprised to find yourself chatting with someone in India. Why? Because India has become an important source of workers for American companies!

In the 1990s, many companies decided to focus on what they did best (like making computers) and find partners to handle other parts of their business (like customer service calls). To accomplish this, they hired outside service companies to perform jobs such as:

- accounting
- help for computer problems
- processing medical forms
- customer service
- processing insurance forms
- security

This practice became known as "outsourcing." A number of smart business people in Bangalore, India realized the great opportunities that outsourcing provided! They began to offer business services that were less expensive than any other competitor in the world. They could do this because India's economy was weak and Indians would work for very low wages.

Today, Bangalore is considered to be the outsourcing capital of India. Bangalore companies provide business services around the world!

Did you know?
Bangalore is called the "Silicon Valley" of India, because it is the nation's leading information technology employer and exporter!

Figure it out!

List six business functions that could be outsourced.

Why Be "Sari"?

Have you ever seen an Indian woman dressed in a beautiful dress? The *sari*, or *saree*, is the traditional garment for females in India. A *sari* consists of several yards of lightweight cloth, usually cotton or linen, which is draped over the body so that one end forms a skirt and the other a shoulder or head covering. The word *sari* comes from the Sanskrit word *sati*, or cloth.

Wealthy women in the upper levels of the caste system wear more elaborate and fashionable *saris* made of fine silk and complemented by a variety of silver or gold jewelry.

Today, *saris* can be seen in many parts of the western world and are worn in many cultures. Designs, patterns, and even the styles for wearing a *sari* may have changed over time, but it remains one of the most exquisite single-piece garments for any woman who wants to look and feel elegant!

Dress Up!

Help Christina get dressed for her tour of India! Here are some of the clothing styles you could see in India today. Choose which outfit she'll wear. Color the clothing, and draw a line from the piece of clothing to Christina or cut the clothing out and dress her up!

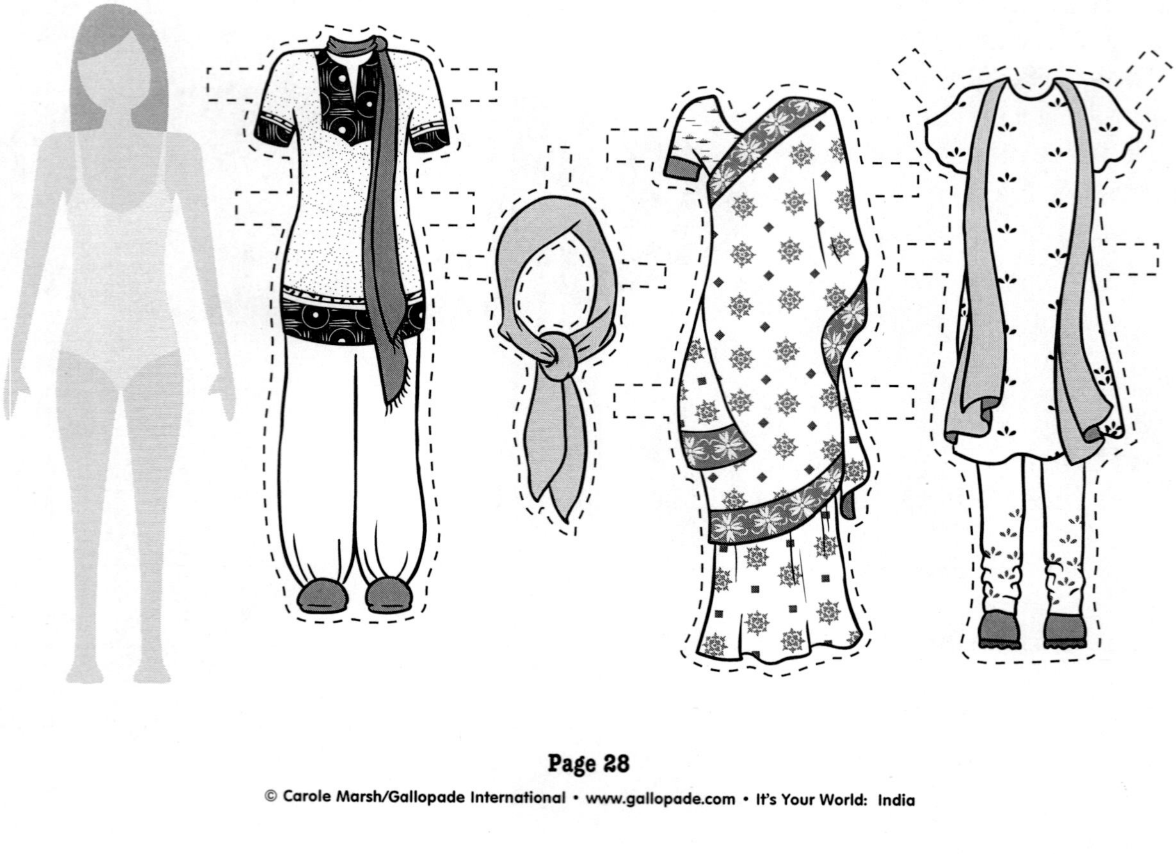

Assorted Architecture!

Figure it out!
Use the following clues to figure out this famous structure in Ranakpur, India.

- This temple is the largest Jain temple in India.
- The Hindus that worship here are known for absolute nonviolence.
- The 1444 columns are each made of one piece of marble and richly decorated.
- No two columns in the temple are alike.
- The temple was built in the 15th century.
- As light shifts through the temple throughout the day, the column colors change from white to blue to gold.

1.

4.

2.

3.

6.

5.

Is It from India?

Here are a few English words that originated from the Hindi and Sanskrit Indian languages!

bandana: a scarf that is tied around the head or neck

bangle: a type of bracelet

bungalow: term for a type of house

candy: sugar

cash: coins or paper money

cot: a portable bed

emerald: a type of precious stone

ginger: a spice

guru: a teacher

jungle: wilderness or forest

karma: acts or deeds

lilac: a type of flower

loot: goods or money

mugger: street robber

opal: a type of precious stone

rice: a type of grain

sentry: an armed guard

shampoo: a hair cleanser

shawl: a strip of cloth

thug: thief

Can you find more?

____

____

____

____

Further Resources

U.S. Embassy in India
Shantipath, Chanakyapuri
New Delhi - 110021
Phone: 011-2419-8000
Fax: +91-11-2419-0017

United Nations
2 United Nations Plaza
New York, NY 10017

India Tourism Office
1270, Avenue of Americas, Suite 1808, 18th Floor
New York, NY 10020 USA
Phone: +1-212-586-4901/ 4902 /4903
Fax: +1-212-582-3274

Interesting Websites

http://www.incredibleindia.org

http://www.tourindia.com

http://www.bollywood.com

http://www.sacredindia.com

Answer Key

Page 7
1. flag 2. population 3. vegetarian 4. Hindu
5. movie 6. garments

Page 8
1. d 2. c

Page 9

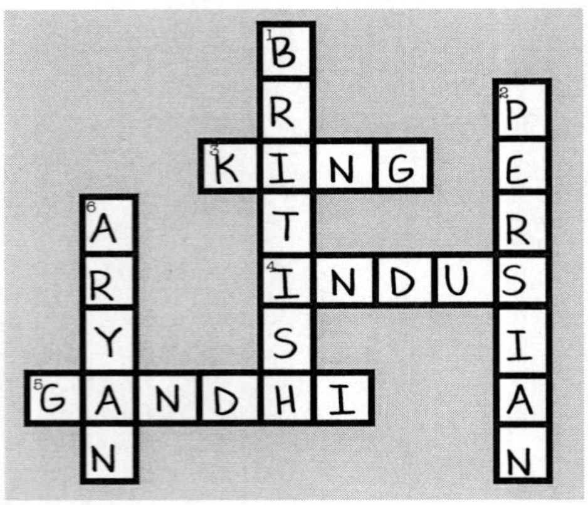

Page 10
1, 4, 2, 6, 7, 3, 5

Page 11
1.E, 2. C, 3. F, 4. B, 5. D, 6. A

Page 12
Drought -B, City Overcrowding -D,
Black Plague - A, Ubhas Chandra Bose - E, Cows Thought to be Relatives - C

Page 17
badan - rice
munh - mouth
naam - name
haath - hand
tamatar - tomato
lamba - long
upar - above
din - day
bara - big
suraj - sun

Page 21
1. 14 minutes
2. 6 players (3+3)

Page 22
Temple/Mosque - Mahalaxmi Temple, Haji Ali Mausoleum, Siddhivinayak Temple
Historical/Nature - Hanging Gardens, Sanjay Gandhi National Park
Museum - Nehru Planetarium, Prince of Wales Museum

Page 25
mangrove

Page 26
Hydapes

Page 27
accounting, customer service, help for computer problems, processing insurance forms, processing medical forms, security

Page 29
Jain Temple Ranakpur